# Dinos

Written by Rachel Griffiths
and Margaret Clyne
Illustrated by Sharyn Madder

HORWITZ
MARTIN
EDUCATION

A long time ago,
there were many kinds
of dinosaurs.

Some dinosaurs
ate plants.

These dinosaurs
ate plants.
They had blunt teeth.

Diplodocus

Some dinosaurs
ate meat.

This dinosaur
ate meat.
It had sharp teeth.

Tyrannosaurus rex

Some dinosaurs
could fly.

This dinosaur
could fly.
It had wings.

Archaeopteryx

Some dinosaurs
could swim.

These dinosaurs
could swim.
They had flippers.

Ichthyosaurs

11

Some dinosaurs
could walk on two legs.

These dinosaurs
could walk on two legs.

Iguanodons

Some dinosaurs
could walk on four legs.

This dinosaur
could walk on four legs.

Triceratops

15

|  | Diplodocus | Tyrannosaurus rex | Archaeopteryx | Ichthyosaur | Iguanodon | Triceratops |
|---|---|---|---|---|---|---|
|  | | | | | | |
| Walked on four legs | ● |  |  |  |  | ● |
| Walked on two legs |  | ● | ● |  | ● |  |
| Ate meat |  | ● | ● | ● |  |  |
| Ate plants | ● |  |  |  | ● | ● |
| Flew |  |  | ● |  |  |  |
| Swam |  |  |  | ● |  |  |

16